THE
POSSIBILITY
PROJECT

THE
POSSIBILITY
PROJECT

a guided journal for
creating what's possible

Erin Cummings

TO KYLE, FOR ALWAYS REMINDING ME
THAT I AM TRULY CAPABLE OF CREATING
WHAT IS POSSIBLE.

TO YOU, FOR TRULY KNOWING THAT YOU
ARE CAPABLE, TOO.

Library of Congress Cataloging-in-Publication Data
available.

ISBN: 978-1-68555-028-8

Manufactured in China.

Design by Andrea Kelly.
Typesetting by AJ Hansen.

10 9 8 7 6 5 4 3 2 1

The Collective Book Studio®
Oakland, California
www.thecollectivebook.studio

Table OF CONTENTS

> **"CEASE TO HOPE, AND YOU WILL CEASE TO FEAR."**
>
> —HECATO (SENECA, *MORAL LETTERS*, 5.7B–8)

I stopped pretending to believe in myself a while ago, and I started showing myself what I'm actually capable of so that I didn't have to pretend to believe anymore.

I'll say it, "F*ck hope."

I don't think "hope" is bad; I just realized it's not for me any-more. Hope brought want, which led to worry. I've had a lot of shit happen in my life, and the worry eats me alive. The worry gave me PTSD when my dad was in the hospital after his mo-torcycle accident in 2019, the worry gave me loss of clients and community when the COVID-19 pandemic hit the yoga studio that I own in 2020, the worry gave me a toxic relationship with my family from whom I've now distanced myself, and the worry keeps me in bed with my covers over my head. The worry is suffocating.

We are multifaceted human beings. Our past shapes our present, and our actions shape our future.

What if you stopped hoping for what you want to have happen and started getting present to what's possible, not through hope, but what you're actually capable of doing?

What if you didn't just manifest things, what if you didn't just set goals, what if you actually looked at how you feel, where you are focused, and how needing constant bursts of motivation impacts your life?

A few years ago I was diagnosed with PTSD. I told no one, and needed to make major life changes. There is no room for hope in that equation. I had to realize that the situation I was in was not okay and that I was not okay. Getting present to realizing what was happening brought me back to what I can control instead of just hoping everything would be okay.

The only way to manage a PTSD episode is through presence, and once I got present I started seeing what was possible. I started focusing on four areas of my life that incorporated my whole self. I could be a mom and a business owner. I could have a mental health issue and be productive. I could actually be multifaceted because it's all possible.

The biggest thing yoga has taught me over the years is that through presence, possibility exists. Hope doesn't fit that equation either.

So, I made my own equation that I'm so excited to share with you, the Possibility Project: A place to create what's possible through productivity, creativity, movement, and purpose. A place to get present so you know what you are capable of so that you don't have to pretend anymore.

You are courageous. You are capable. You are strong. It's time for you to create what's possible.

Erin Cummings

vision

> "VISION WITHOUT EXECUTION IS DELUSION."
> —THOMAS EDISON

In order to shift from hope to creating what's possible, you need to get present. This first section is all about the vision of your life and how you see it. Take your time filling out these next few pages. If you have a meditation practice, meditating before you answer these journal questions is a great way to support this journaling exercise.

Real talk, there is no way to move purposely forward without knowing what you actually want. Get detailed and clear about what you see in your life so that you have a vision of not only your life as a whole, but also what's possible.

Your vision will be important in realizing what you actually want. If you don't wake up to what you want, if you don't wake up to realize what's already working in your life, if you don't wake up to what exhausts you, you'll keep staying asleep to opportunities that come your way.

If you're like me, your mind is always moving, always thinking about what's next. That's why I love the idea of seeing what's possible as a project. You can bring into view many possibilities or one big possibility, but either way you have a clear path you are working toward.

It's time to bring your time frame into focus. Once you have an understanding of how long your project will take, you'll be able to truly commit to this journal in a way that works best for you. Without digging into this journal too much, you already know in your gut what you want and what you want to work toward. You might even already be able to picture it. If not, that is okay too; there's space for both possibilities here.

A great place to start is committing to ninety days. If you know that time frame will not work for your project or if that makes you feel anxious or brought up some tension in your neck, pick a new time frame you know you can commit to. Whether it is ninety days, six months, one year, or a time frame that only you will know, use this journal when needed and find someone who can help you stay accountable to your commitments.

As you move through this journal, you'll be able to customize your experience so that your project can truly fit into your life and into this journal, and this journal can fit in your bag so you can use it when you need it, so that you are ready for what's possible.

MY PROJECT IS POSSIBLE TO COMPLETE BY:

....

What about this journal spoke to me?

....

....

....

....

....

What's at stake for me if everything stays the same?

....

....

....

....

....

What do I really want?

....

....

....

....

....

What is possible if I had no limitations?

....

....

....

....

....

What do I want to accomplish within my established time frame?

....

....

....

....

....

What can I accomplish within my established time frame if I believe in myself?

....

....

....

....

....

What is working in my life right now?

....

....

....

....

....

What is not working in my life right now?

....

....

....

....

....

Where do I feel the most stuck?

....

....

....

....

What in my life excites me the most?

....

....

....

....

....

What in my life exhausts me the most?

....

....

....

....

....

What in my life gives me purpose?

....

....

....

....

Write down what's possible thirty days from completing this project.

....

....

....

....

....

....

....

What advice would future me give?

....

....

....

....

....

....

....

create what's possible

"WHEN YOU BECOME COMFORTABLE WITH UNCERTAINTY, INFINITE POSSIBILITIES OPEN UP IN YOUR LIFE."
—ECKHART TOLLE

You've seen what's possible through vision; now it's time to create it. This section is all about getting your ideas on paper, creating your goals, and then working on action-based tasks to get you where you want to go.

You probably picked up this journal because you feel stuck, tired, and maybe even a little depleted and you know deep down inside that something is there ready to come to life!

This is where you can't rely only on hope; you have to start making things happen for yourself whether they are big goals or small goals.

This section will help you not only keep your vision clear, but also create a pathway for you to get to where you want to go. Over the next few pages you will define how productivity, creativity, movement, and purpose fulfill your life, create a mind map of each of these areas, and set your goals so that you can move into the daily work of making what you want possible.

Once again, doing this type of journaling after a meditation practice is a great way to battle all those *I should have / would have / could have* thoughts that might pop up. If you don't have a meditation practice and struggle with a self-deprecating inner voice, look to your vision of where you are going to help keep you present and focused.

CREATE CLARITY

This journal has four areas of focus: Productivity, Creativity, Movement, and Purpose. In order to create what's possible, let's get clear on how each of these categories are defined for you.

Write your definition of each category or write the most important things you value about that category and how they add fulfillment to your life. Once you are able to define how each area of focus works for you, then you can create ideas and goals and work toward what's possible in each area.

define PRODUCTIVITY

Example: Productivity consists of action-based items I do on purpose to add value to my day without drowning in to-do lists. Action-based items that make me feel productive are meal planning, taking days off, meditation, blocking off calendar times, intentional rest, etc.

....

....

....

....

....

....

....

....

....

define CREATIVITY

If you find yourself saying, "I'm not a creative person," think about all the things that give you inspiration. This definition is not about who you are as a person, but how your imagination shows up in your life.

....

....

....

....

....

....

....

....

....

....

....

....

....

....

....

....

....

define MOVEMENT

This is intentional movement. This is noticing-how-you-feel-after-you-work-out kind of movement. If you know doing a sixty-minute heavy cardio workout makes you feel like crap, do not write that down. What intention-based movement makes you feel fulfilled? It can be anything from yoga to ten minutes of walking outside.

define PURPOSE

Think about your core values that you use to center yourself and your decisions. This is not about making more money or having more things, but ways to create joy and fulfillment through empowering yourself and others.

MIND MAPPING

The best way to brainstorm is to start with a clear purpose.

Mind mapping is a great way to start without feeling over-whelmed, and it's the perfect first step, especially when you don't know what the end will actually look like.

HERE'S HOW IT WORKS:

On the next two pages, you will see a mind map. Everything is sectioned into four main categories: Productivity, Creativity, Movement, and Purpose. In each category, you will write four things that you are already doing or things you are striving for. You may even need to use those ideas to create subtopics.

The process of mind mapping helps simplify, organize, and give your ideas connection and context.

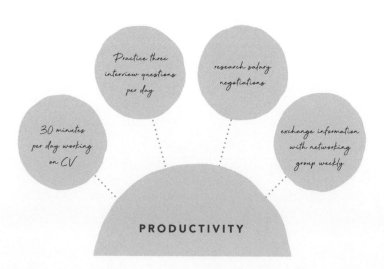

PUT YOUR THOUGHTS ON PAPER:

In order to best use this tool, pick one main category at a time (such as Productivity), and list four things that are already working in your life that you could sustainably continue to do, or know that you could potentially do in the future and go from there.

There are a few different ways to look at this. Here are two examples:

1. You can separate them into subcategories like Work, School, Morning Routine, Evening Routine, Use Google Calendar, then within each, write more ideas. Underneath "Work," you might write "Categorize days for optimal productivity," or underneath "Use Google Calendar" write "Block off exercise time, set reminders and links for meal planning."

2. Get straight to the point. Maybe you are looking at finding a new job. You could write "thirty minutes per day working on CV, practice three interview questions per day, research salary negotiations, exchange information with networking group weekly."

If you write these in keywords or in the affirmative, it will be easier to spark action and track progress in the future.

PRODUCTIVITY

CREATIVITY

MOVEMENT

PURPOSE

GOALS

Now that you know where you are going, let's focus on the *how* of getting there. This is where you don't need hope. You need clear and precise actions to move you toward the path you actually desire, and you want to know why you are on that path.

Those actions are your goals.

For each category (Productivity, Creativity, Movement, and Purpose), you will create *three main goals* and up to five supporting goals that will help move you forward and keep you on track.

Using your mind map from the previous page, set SMART goals that have a realistic time frame that you know will challenge you but not overwhelm you. If you have goals that are one to five years out, use those as your main goals, and create supporting goals that have shorter time frames.

SMART goals are defined as the following:

SPECIFIC: Goals are detailed and you can answer questions like "who, what, when, where, why, and which."

MEASURABLE: Goals can be measured or tracked, as in there is a defined answer if a goal was achieved or not.

ACHIEVABLE: Goals are realistic and stay in the realm of possibility.

RELEVANT: Goals are worthwhile and align with other goals you are working toward.

TIME-BOUND: Goals have an end-by date.

Write each main goal in the affirmative and add the purpose behind your goal. Example: "I am on my third job interview, actively pursuing a new accounts manager position by November 2 so that I can be part of the leadership team and bring more diversity and empowerment to our workplace."

If you are working on losing weight as a goal or saving money for a trip, that is a great place to start! Take some time to think about what you are really getting out of losing that twenty extra pounds or what you ultimately want to get out of going on that trip. See yourself as courageous, strong, and capable, then write your goals!

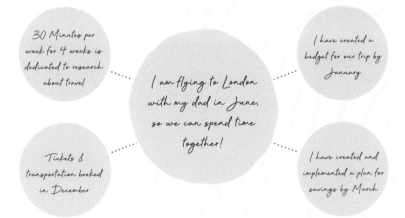

30 Minutes per week for 4 weeks is dedicated to research about travel

I am flying to London with my dad in June, so we can spend time together!

I have created a budget for our trip by January

Tickets & transportation booked in December

I have created and implemented a plan for savings by March

Productivity
GOALS

Keep in mind that productivity includes time
for rest and recharging. Keep it simple—focus
on the thoughts that come up first.

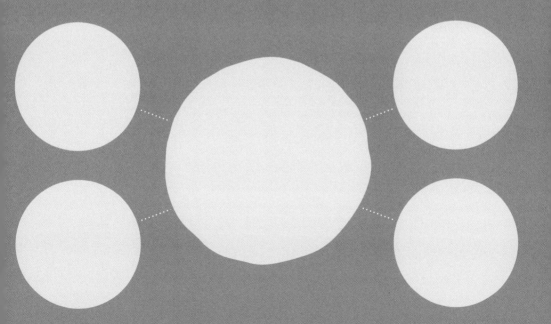

Creativity
GOALS

Tell yourself, "I am creative." Remember,
creativity can also focus on what inspires you
and sparks imagination.

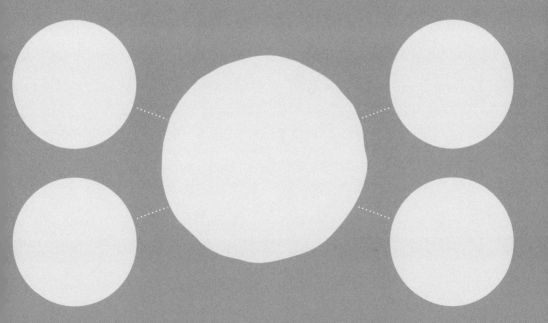

Movement
GOALS

Think realistically, movement is more than CrossFit snatches and full marathons. Meditative walks and five-minute morning stretches are just as important.

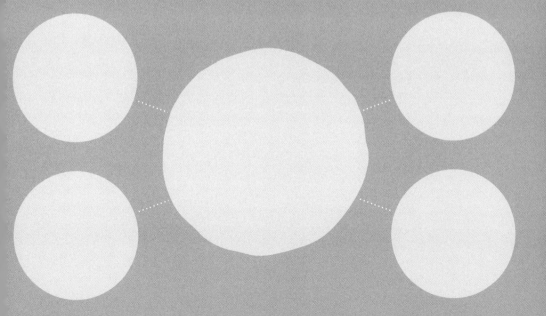

Purpose
GOALS

These goals light your heart on fire and fill your cup to the brim! Put your hand on your heart and ask yourself what goals will light up the world around you.

One action I need to take to move forward with my goals is:

....

....

....

Assumptions I am making about not being able to complete my goals:

....

....

....

....

....

....

Assumptions I am making about completing my goals:

....

....

....

....

....

....

Once my goals are accomplished, I will be grateful for:

....

....

....

....

....

Once my goals are accomplished, I will feel:

....

....

....

....

....

Knowing my goals do not define me, I am choosing:

....

....

....

....

....

truth

> "ONE ACCURATE MEASUREMENT IS WORTH
> A THOUSAND EXPERT OPINIONS."
> —GRACE HOPPER

Hope places control into somebody or something else's hands. When you become present, you realize what you are actually capable of doing and what you are capable of controlling at that moment.

In this section, be honest with yourself and come from a place of neutrality. Think of this section like data. You might know where you want to go, but we need a starting point or at least some guidelines along the way.

You'll see the truth about how you are actually spending your time rather than just hoping you'll start to spend your time wisely.

You'll get clear in this section about how you spend your time and how you feel during that time.

Once you realize at what time you are most productive, what time of day feels best to move your body, and when you need to give yourself extra rest, you can move into a space of flow instead of being exhausted from motivational bursts.

THE HOW

If your life is already hard, these next two days will continue to be. Honestly, these next two days might be the most challenging part of this journal. This process is not difficult because it takes a lot of work, but because you need to work through these next two days through nonjudgmental awareness.

All you have to do is write it down. Don't make it wrong; don't make it right. Don't use the dreaded *I should have done this* phrase. Stop it. View this as data. Keep it all neutral.

You will use the left timetable to write down actions or "doings" you did that day. On the right side, you will write how you *feel* for each action.

If you do any part of the program, this is the part to do. Putting all this on paper can help you analyze when during the day you feel a certain way, what action made you feel that way, when your most productive and creative times of the day are, and when you need a rest break.

From this data, you can completely change your schedule to working on your to-do list during your productivity hours, and working on your creativity during creativity hours. It will also show you when you need rest or active rest during the day, and when the best time to intentionally move your body is based on how you feel and what you need.

Don't forget you might have all the data you need to start living a perfectly productive life, but that's the thing with productivity . . . it's a practice. You will never perfect it, something will always come up, but if you are prepared, productivity gets easier and you can start to focus on what you really want.

Time	Activity	Feeling
6:00 A.M.	wake up	exhausted
6:30 A.M.	eat breakfast/make kid lunches / get ready	hopeful
7:00 P.M.	walk to school	grounded / happy
7:30 P.M.	yell at my kid for forgetting homework	angry / shame
8:00 P.M.	drive to work	guilty / lonely
8:30 P.M.	clean yoga studio	tired
9:00 P.M.	get coffee from the coffee shop	tired
9:30 P.M.	start on payroll	valued
10:00 P.M.	balance studio checkbook	determined
10:30 P.M.	write blog	inspired
11:00 P.M.	write a recipe	inspired
11:30 P.M.		
12:00 P.M.		
12:30 P.M.		
1:00 P.M.		
1:30 P.M.		
2:00 P.M.		
2:30 P.M.		

DATE: ....

	I DID:	I FELT:

6:00 A.M. ....

6:30 A.M. ....

7:00 A.M. ....

7:30 A.M. ....

8:00 A.M. ....

8:30 A.M. ....

9:00 A.M. ....

9:30 A.M. ....

10:00 A.M. ....

10:30 A.M. ....

11:00 A.M. ....

11:30 A.M. ....

12:00 P.M. ....

NOTES

12:30 P.M. ....

1:00 P.M. ....

1:30 P.M. ....

2:00 P.M. ....

2:30 P.M. ....

3:00 P.M. ....

3:30 P.M. ....

4:00 P.M. ....

4:30 P.M. ....

5:00 P.M. ....

5:30 P.M. ....

6:00 P.M. ....

6:30 P.M. ....

7:00 P.M. ....

7:30 P.M. ....

8:00 P.M. ....

8:30 P.M. ....

9:00 P.M. ....

GET PRESENT

I am most productive during the hours of:

....

....

....

I am most creative during the hours of:

....

....

....

My body feels best when I move during the hours of:

....

....

....

I need rest during the hours of:
(NOTICE WHEN YOU FEEL TIRED/BORED DURING THE DAY, NOT JUST FOR SLEEP!)

....

....

....

....

MAKE AN IMPACT

I am able to prioritize my schedule by:

....

....

....

....

....

....

The shifts I need to make in my habits and calendar are:

....

....

....

....

....

....

....

DATE: ....

	I DID:	I FELT:

6:00 A.M. ....

6:30 A.M. ....

7:00 A.M. ....

7:30 A.M. ....

8:00 A.M. ....

8:30 A.M. ....

9:00 A.M. ....

9:30 A.M. ....

10:00 A.M. ....

10:30 A.M. ....

11:00 A.M. ....

11:30 A.M. ....

12:00 P.M. ....

NOTES

12:30 P.M. ....

1:00 P.M. ....

1:30 P.M. ....

2:00 P.M. ....

2:30 P.M. ....

3:00 P.M. ....

3:30 P.M. ....

4:00 P.M. ....

4:30 P.M. ....

5:00 P.M. ....

5:30 P.M. ....

6:00 P.M. ....

6:30 P.M. ....

7:00 P.M. ....

7:30 P.M. ....

8:00 P.M. ....

8:30 P.M. ....

9:00 P.M. ....

GET PRESENT

I am most productive during the hours of:

....

....

....

I am most creative during the hours of:

....

....

....

My body feels best when I move during the hours of:

....

....

....

I need rest during the hours of:

(NOTICE WHEN YOU FEEL TIRED/BORED DURING THE DAY, NOT JUST FOR SLEEP!)

....

....

....

....

MAKE AN IMPACT

I am able to prioritize my schedule by:

....

....

....

....

....

....

....

The shifts I need to make in my habits and calendar are:

....

....

....

....

....

....

....

"CLARITY IS POWER. THE MORE CLEAR YOU ARE ABOUT WHAT YOU WANT, THE MORE LIKELY YOU ARE TO ACHIEVE IT."
—BILLY COX

If you don't know what you really want, if you don't know what your goals are, if you don't know actionable ways to stay on your path, then you are just asking for luck. You might as well just hope you get lucky, and that's the exact opposite of what this journal is about.

This section is all about clarity. Using all the work you did in the previous sections creates the groundwork for moving into creating what's possible.

Moving forward, you will journal and set yourself up for the week or month or whichever time frame you want to have. Our focus and vision moves from the future to the week ahead and then to the day you want to have. This keeps you on a direct path moving forward, and if you veer off from the path you won't have to go far to redirect yourself.

This is an opportunity to get clear about how you want your week and your days to look so when failure, questioning yourself, and the inevitable craziness of nothing going right show up, you are prepared and grounded in what you need and what you know.

The Time Frame I Want

THIS SECTION IS POSSIBLE TO COMPLETE BY:

....

DAYS - WEEKS - MONTHS

My three goals are:

- ....
- ....
- ....

The three most essential things I need to complete are:

- ....
- ....
- ....

The project that's possible:

....

....

....

....

CREATIVE UNTANGLING

The challenges I'm facing:

I can ask for help with:

Assumptions I'm making are:

BE INTENTIONAL

I want to feel:

....

EMOTION

My body needs:

....

....

....

....

I sabotage feeling the way I want by:

....

....

....

....

CLARITY THROUGH FULFILLMENT

The best ways to take care of myself this week are:

- ....

- ....

- ....

CREATE PURPOSE

Write what it's like at the end of this week:

WHAT DID YOU COMPLETE AND HOW ARE YOU CELEBRATING?

Use this grid to plan, organize, create, or unravel
whatever is needed for your projected time frame.

THINGS LIKE: MENU PLANNING, GROCERY LISTS, BUDGETING, GARDEN NOTES.
ANYTHING YOU NEED TO MOVE FROM CHAOS TO CREATION GOES HERE.

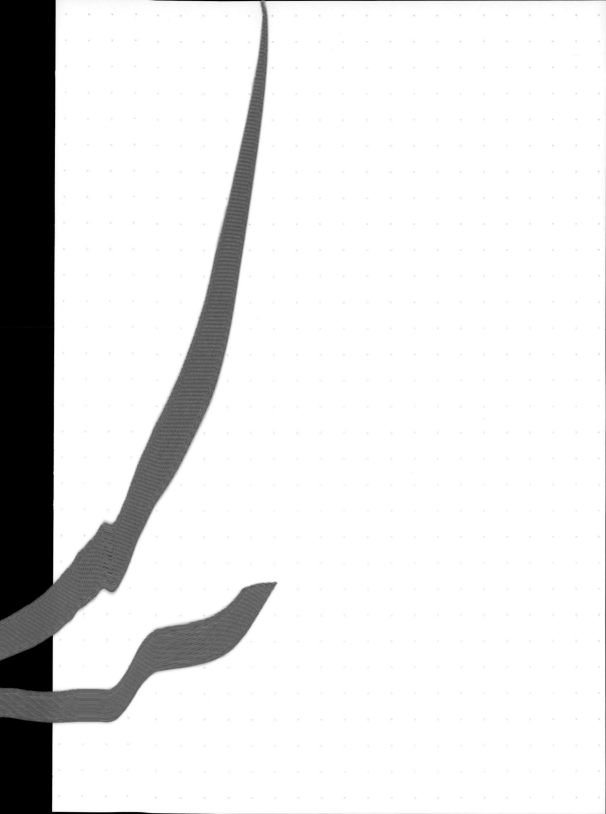

Today

Today's intention:

....

....

GET PRODUCTIVE

This isn't your normal "to-do" list. To-do lists are limitless. This list is a finite version of what you *will actually* accomplish today. Practice writing what you know you will accomplish, not all the things you need to accomplish. On the hard days, you can write "brushed teeth," "took a shower," "called Grandma." This list should be clear and concise.

- ....
- ....
- ....
- ....
- ....
- ....
- ....
- ....

GET CREATIVE

I have an idea:

What will hold me back:

What I know is true:

One action I can take:

CONTINUE *Today* →

GET MOVING

I went to bed feeling:

....

....

....

I woke up feeling:

....

....

....

Moving made me feel:

....

MOVEMENT TYPE

DEPLETED   **FULL**

EMOTION TO ACTION

When I felt:

....

....

....

....

....

....

....

Action I took:

....

....

....

....

....

....

....

GET PURPOSEFUL

Today's affirmation:

....

....

Review your day from neutrality

WHAT WORKED:

- ....

- ....

- ....

- ....

- ....

- ....

- ....

- ....

WHAT DIDN'T WORK:

- ....

- ....

- ....

- ....

- ....

- ....

- ....

- ....

My new choice:

LOOKING AT YOUR VISION AND YOUR GOALS, WHAT IS A NEW CHOICE THAT YOU CAN MAKE MOVING FORWARD TO GIVE YOURSELF A NEW CHANCE FOR POSSIBILITY?

....

....

Today

Today's intention:

....
....
....

GET PRODUCTIVE

Today I will:

- ....
- ....
- ....
- ....
- ....
- ....
- ....
- ....
- ....

GET CREATIVE

I have an idea:

What will hold me back:

What I know is true:

One action I can take:

CONTINUE *Today* →

GET MOVING

I went to bed feeling:

....

....

....

I woke up feeling:

....

....

....

Moving made me feel:

....

MOVEMENT TYPE

DEPLETED   FULL

EMOTION TO ACTION

When I felt:

Action I took:

....

....

....

....

....

....

....

GET PURPOSEFUL

Today's affirmation:

....

....

Review your day from neutrality

WHAT WORKED:

- ....

- ....

- ....

- ....

- ....

- ....

- ....

- ....

WHAT DIDN'T WORK:

- ....

- ....

- ....

- ....

- ....

- ....

- ....

- ....

My new choice:

....

....

....

Today

....

Today's intention:

....

....

....

GET PRODUCTIVE

Today I will:

- ....

- ....

- ....

- ....

- ....

- ....

- ....

- ....

- ....

GET CREATIVE

I have an idea:

What will hold me back:

What I know is true:

One action I can take:

CONTINUE *Today* →

GET MOVING

I went to bed feeling:

....

....

....

I woke up feeling:

....

....

....

Moving made me feel:

....

MOVEMENT TYPE

DEPLETED   FULL

EMOTION TO ACTION

When I felt:

....

....

....

....

....

....

....

....

Action I took:

....

....

....

....

....

....

....

....

GET PURPOSEFUL

Today's affirmation:

....

....

Review your day from neutrality

WHAT WORKED:

- ....
- ....
- ....
- ....
- ....
- ....
- ....
- ....

WHAT DIDN'T WORK:

- ....
- ....
- ....
- ....
- ....
- ....
- ....
- ....

My new choice:

....

....

....

Today

Today's intention:

....

....

....

GET PRODUCTIVE

Today I will:

- ....
- ....
- ....
- ....
- ....
- ....
- ....
- ....
- ....

GET CREATIVE

I have an idea:

What will hold me back:

What I know is true:

One action I can take:

CONTINUE *Today* →

GET MOVING

I went to bed feeling:

....

....

....

I woke up feeling:

....

....

....

Moving made me feel:

....

MOVEMENT TYPE

DEPLETED   FULL

EMOTION TO ACTION

When I felt:

....

....

....

....

....

....

....

Action I took:

....

....

....

....

....

....

....

GET PURPOSEFUL

Today's affirmation:

....

....

Review your day from neutrality

WHAT WORKED:

- ....
- ....
- ....
- ....
- ....
- ....
- ....
- ....

WHAT DIDN'T WORK:

- ....
- ....
- ....
- ....
- ....
- ....
- ....
- ....

My new choice:

....

....

....

Today

Today's intention:

....

....

....

GET PRODUCTIVE

Today I will:

- ....
- ....
- ....
- ....
- ....
- ....
- ....
- ....
- ....

GET CREATIVE

I have an idea:

What will hold me back:

What I know is true:

One action I can take:

CONTINUE *Today* →

GET MOVING

I went to bed feeling:

....

....

....

I woke up feeling:

....

....

Moving made me feel:

....

MOVEMENT TYPE

DEPLETED   FULL

EMOTION TO ACTION

When I felt:

Action I took:

....

....

....

....

....

....

....

GET PURPOSEFUL

Today's affirmation:

....

....

Review your day from neutrality

WHAT WORKED:

- ....
- ....
- ....
- ....
- ....
- ....
- ....
- ....

WHAT DIDN'T WORK:

- ....
- ....
- ....
- ....
- ....
- ....
- ....
- ....

My new choice:

....

....

....

Today

....

Today's intention:

....

....

....

GET PRODUCTIVE

Today I will:

- ....
- ....
- ....
- ....
- ....
- ....
- ....
- ....
- ....

GET CREATIVE

I have an idea:

What will hold me back:

What I know is true:

One action I can take:

CONTINUE *Today* →

GET MOVING

I went to bed feeling:

....

....

....

I woke up feeling:

....

....

....

Moving made me feel:

....

MOVEMENT TYPE

DEPLETED   FULL

EMOTION TO ACTION

When I felt:

....

....

....

....

....

....

....

Action I took:

....

....

....

....

....

....

....

GET PURPOSEFUL

Today's affirmation:

....

....

Review your day from neutrality

WHAT WORKED:

WHAT DIDN'T WORK:

- ....
- ....
- ....
- ....
- ....
- ....
- ....
- ....

- ....
- ....
- ....
- ....
- ....
- ....
- ....
- ....

My new choice:

....

....

....

Today

....

Today's intention:

....
....
....

GET PRODUCTIVE

Today I will:

- ....
- ....
- ....
- ....
- ....
- ....
- ....
- ....
- ....

GET CREATIVE

I have an idea:

What will hold me back:

What I know is true:

One action I can take:

CONTINUE *Today* →

GET MOVING

I went to bed feeling:

....

....

....

I woke up feeling:

....

....

....

Moving made me feel:

....

MOVEMENT TYPE

DEPLETED   FULL

EMOTION TO ACTION

When I felt:

Action I took:

....

....

....

....

....

....

....

GET PURPOSEFUL

Today's affirmation:

....

....

Review your day from neutrality

WHAT WORKED:

- ....
- ....
- ....
- ....
- ....
- ....
- ....
- ....

WHAT DIDN'T WORK:

- ....
- ....
- ....
- ....
- ....
- ....
- ....
- ....

My new choice:

....

....

....

CELEBRATE THE WINS

I ACHIEVED:

- ....
- ....
- ....
- ....

I TOOK CARE OF MYSELF BY:

- ....
- ....
- ....
- ....

I AM GRATEFUL FOR:

- ....
- ....
- ....
- ....

STEPS I TOOK THIS WEEK THAT HELPED ME ACHIEVE MY GOALS:

- ....
- ....
- ....
- ....

I learned:

....

....

....

CREATE WHOLENESS

This time I feel:

....

....

EMOTION

DEPLETED

FULL

I struggled with:

What I know is true:

I AM PRODUCTIVE.

I AM CREATIVE.

I MOVE WITH PURPOSE.

I LIVE WITH INTENTION.

After saying these affirmations, I am clear about:

....

....

....

....

....

....

....

....

Based on this section's theme of clarity, think about what came into focus this time for you. What are you really clear about moving toward?

....

....

....

....

....

....

....

....

"DESTRUCTION IS ESSENTIAL TO CONSTRUCTION.
IF WE WANT TO BUILD THE NEW,
WE MUST BE WILLING TO LET THE OLD BURN."
—GLENNON DOYLE

Think about taking a match or lighter to an old thought, an old way of thinking, an old way of being, or an old habit and lighting it on fire. This section isn't about burning bridges, it's about starting fresh and renewed because you have clarity. You can now burn down or get rid of what no longer serves you.

Light little conceptual fires in your head, and burn down no longer asking for help, sabotaging your success, not taking care of yourself, or whatever is coming up for you. It will take practice, but burn down the inner voice that says *You can't do it* or *I don't have time for this*.

This is an essential step of moving into what's possible because it creates room for growth without old residue.

The Time Frame I Want

My three goals are:

- ....
- ....
- ....

The three most essential things I need to complete are:

- ....
- ....
- ....

The project that's possible:

....

....

....

....

....

CREATIVE UNTANGLING

The challenges I'm facing:

I can ask for help with:

Assumptions I'm making are:

BE INTENTIONAL

I want to feel:

....

EMOTION

My body needs:

....

....

....

....

I sabotage feeling the way I want by:

....

....

....

....

CLARITY THROUGH FULFILLMENT

The best ways to take care of myself this week are:

- ....

- ....

- ....

CREATE PURPOSE

Write what it's like at the end of this week:

WHAT DID YOU COMPLETE, WHAT DID YOU CONCEPTUALLY BURN, AND HOW ARE YOU CELEBRATING?

Use this grid to plan, organize, create, or unravel
whatever is needed for your projected time frame.

THINGS LIKE: MENU PLANNING, GROCERY LISTS, BUDGETING, GARDEN NOTES.
ANYTHING YOU NEED TO MOVE FROM CHAOS TO CREATION GOES HERE.

Today

....

Today's intention:

....

....

....

GET PRODUCTIVE

Today I will:

- ....
- ....
- ....
- ....
- ....
- ....
- ....
- ....
- ....

GET CREATIVE

I have an idea:

What will hold me back:

What I know is true:

One action I can take:

CONTINUE *Today* →

GET MOVING

I went to bed feeling:

....

....

....

I woke up feeling:

....

....

....

Moving made me feel:

....

MOVEMENT TYPE

DEPLETED   FULL

EMOTION TO ACTION

When I felt:

....

....

....

....

....

....

....

Action I took:

....

....

....

....

....

....

....

GET PURPOSEFUL

Today's affirmation:

....

....

Review your day from neutrality

WHAT WORKED:

- ....
- ....
- ....
- ....
- ....
- ....
- ....
- ....

WHAT DIDN'T WORK:

- ....
- ....
- ....
- ....
- ....
- ....
- ....
- ....

My new choice:

....

....

....

Today

Today's intention:

....

....

....

GET PRODUCTIVE

Today I will:

- ....
- ....
- ....
- ....
- ....
- ....
- ....
- ....
- ....

GET CREATIVE

I have an idea:

What will hold me back:

What I know is true:

One action I can take:

CONTINUE *Today* →

GET MOVING

I went to bed feeling:

....

....

....

I woke up feeling:

....

....

....

Moving made me feel:

....

MOVEMENT TYPE

DEPLETED   **FULL**

EMOTION TO ACTION

When I felt:

....

....

....

....

....

....

....

Action I took:

....

....

....

....

....

....

....

GET PURPOSEFUL

Today's affirmation:

....

....

Review your day from neutrality

WHAT WORKED:

- ....
- ....
- ....
- ....
- ....
- ....
- ....
- ....

WHAT DIDN'T WORK:

- ....
- ....
- ....
- ....
- ....
- ....
- ....
- ....

My new choice:

....

....

....

Today

Today's intention:

....

....

....

GET PRODUCTIVE

Today I will:

- ....
- ....
- ....
- ....
- ....
- ....
- ....
- ....
- ....

GET CREATIVE

I have an idea:

What will hold me back:

What I know is true:

One action I can take:

CONTINUE *Today* →

GET MOVING

I went to bed feeling:

....

....

....

I woke up feeling:

....

....

....

Moving made me feel:

....

MOVEMENT TYPE

DEPLETED   **FULL**

EMOTION TO ACTION

When I felt:

....

....

....

....

....

....

....

Action I took:

....

....

....

....

....

....

....

GET PURPOSEFUL

Today's affirmation:

....

....

Review your day from neutrality

WHAT WORKED:

- ....
- ....
- ....
- ....
- ....
- ....
- ....
- ....

WHAT DIDN'T WORK:

- ....
- ....
- ....
- ....
- ....
- ....
- ....
- ....

My new choice:

....

....

....

Today

Today's intention:

....

....

....

GET PRODUCTIVE

Today I will:

- ....
- ....
- ....
- ....
- ....
- ....
- ....
- ....
- ....

GET CREATIVE

I have an idea:

What will hold me back:

What I know is true:

One action I can take:

GET MOVING

I went to bed feeling:

....

....

....

I woke up feeling:

....

....

....

Moving made me feel:

....

MOVEMENT TYPE

DEPLETED   FULL

EMOTION TO ACTION

When I felt:

....

....

....

....

....

....

....

Action I took:

....

....

....

....

....

....

....

GET PURPOSEFUL

Today's affirmation:

....

....

Review your day from neutrality

WHAT WORKED:

- ....
- ....
- ....
- ....
- ....
- ....
- ....
- ....

WHAT DIDN'T WORK:

- ....
- ....
- ....
- ....
- ....
- ....
- ....
- ....

My new choice:

....

....

....

Today

Today's intention:

....
....
....

GET PRODUCTIVE

Today I will:

- ....
- ....
- ....
- ....
- ....
- ....
- ....
- ....
- ....

GET CREATIVE

I have an idea:

What will hold me back:

What I know is true:

One action I can take:

GET MOVING

I went to bed feeling:

....

....

....

I woke up feeling:

....

....

....

Moving made me feel:

....

MOVEMENT TYPE

DEPLETED   FULL

EMOTION TO ACTION

When I felt:

....

....

....

....

....

....

....

Action I took:

....

....

....

....

....

....

....

GET PURPOSEFUL

Today's affirmation:

....

....

Review your day from neutrality

WHAT WORKED:

- ....
- ....
- ....
- ....
- ....
- ....
- ....
- ....

WHAT DIDN'T WORK:

- ....
- ....
- ....
- ....
- ....
- ....
- ....
- ....

My new choice:

....

....

....

Today

Today's intention:

....
....
....

GET PRODUCTIVE

Today I will:

- ....
- ....
- ....
- ....
- ....
- ....
- ....
- ....
- ....

GET CREATIVE

I have an idea:

What will hold me back:

What I know is true:

One action I can take:

GET MOVING

I went to bed feeling:

....

....

....

I woke up feeling:

....

....

....

Moving made me feel:

....

MOVEMENT TYPE

DEPLETED   FULL

EMOTION TO ACTION

When I felt:

Action I took:

....

....

....

....

....

....

....

GET PURPOSEFUL

Today's affirmation:

....

....

Review your day from neutrality

WHAT WORKED: **WHAT DIDN'T WORK:**

- ....   - ....

- ....   - ....

- ....   - ....

- ....   - ....

- ....   - ....

- ....   - ....

- ....   - ....

- ....   - ....

My new choice:

....

....

....

Today

Today's intention:

....

....

....

GET PRODUCTIVE

Today I will:

- ....
- ....
- ....
- ....
- ....
- ....
- ....
- ....
- ....

GET CREATIVE

I have an idea:

What will hold me back:

What I know is true:

One action I can take:

CONTINUE *Today* →

GET MOVING

I went to bed feeling:

....

....

....

I woke up feeling:

....

....

....

Moving made me feel:

....

MOVEMENT TYPE

DEPLETED   FULL

EMOTION TO ACTION

When I felt:

....

....

....

....

....

....

....

Action I took:

....

....

....

....

....

....

....

GET PURPOSEFUL

Today's affirmation:

....

....

Review your day from neutrality

WHAT WORKED:

- ....
- ....
- ....
- ....
- ....
- ....
- ....
- ....

WHAT DIDN'T WORK:

- ....
- ....
- ....
- ....
- ....
- ....
- ....
- ....

My new choice:

....

....

....

CELEBRATE THE WINS

I ACHIEVED:

- ....
- ....
- ....
- ....

I TOOK CARE OF MYSELF BY:

- ....
- ....
- ....
- ....

I AM GRATEFUL FOR:

- ....
- ....
- ....
- ....

STEPS I TOOK THIS WEEK THAT HELPED ME ACHIEVE MY GOALS:

- ....
- ....
- ....
- ....

I learned:

....
....
....

CREATE WHOLENESS

This time I feel:

....

....

EMOTION

DEPLETED   **FULL**

I struggled with:

What I know is true:

I AM PRODUCTIVE.

I AM CREATIVE.

I MOVE WITH PURPOSE.

I LIVE WITH INTENTION.

After saying these affirmations, the old stuff that I'm willing to burn down is:

....

....

....

....

....

....

....

You've done so much work so far; don't stop. Take a moment to notice how far you've come. From this point in your path, what are you willing to conceptually burn away and move toward? Think about how that renewal will impact your life moving forward.

....

....

....

....

....

....

....

....

light a spark

> "KNOWING EXACTLY WHAT YOU WANT TO DO,
> WITH UNWAVERING CONVICTION IS THE SPARK
> THAT GENERATES EVERYTHING."
> —DEEPAK CHOPRA

You created a focal point for your life, you got clear on a path to get there, you've burned down what was in your way. Now it's time to light a new spark within. The spark you are lighting is full of ambition for possibility.

The friction it takes to strike a match is intentional. Each match you spark is a choice. Practice your new choices this week, and remember each choice is a new opportunity to move forward into your possibility.

You'll start again with your truths of time and emotion. Remember this is from a neutral, data-oriented perspective. No shame, no judgment, just facts. Choose two days this week to collect your truth data while continuing your daily journal entries.

DATE: ....

	I DID:	**I FELT:**

6:00 A.M. ....

6:30 A.M. ....

7:00 A.M. ....

7:30 A.M. ....

8:00 A.M. ....

8:30 A.M. ....

9:00 A.M. ....

9:30 A.M. ....

10:00 A.M. ....

10:30 A.M. ....

11:00 A.M. ....

11:30 A.M. ....

12:00 P.M. ....

NOTES

12:30 P.M. ....

1:00 P.M. ....

1:30 P.M. ....

2:00 P.M. ....

2:30 P.M. ....

3:00 P.M. ....

3:30 P.M. ....

4:00 P.M. ....

4:30 P.M. ....

5:00 P.M. ....

5:30 P.M. ....

6:00 P.M. ....

6:30 P.M. ....

7:00 P.M. ....

7:30 P.M. ....

8:00 P.M. ....

8:30 P.M. ....

9:00 P.M. ....

GET PRESENT

I am most productive during the hours of:

....

....

....

....

I am most creative during the hours of:

....

....

....

My body feels best when I move during the hours of:

....

....

....

I need rest during the hours of:

(NOTICE WHEN YOU FEEL TIRED/BORED DURING THE DAY, NOT JUST FOR SLEEP!)

....

....

....

....

MAKE AN IMPACT

I am able to prioritize my schedule by:

....

....

....

....

I burned down:

....

....

....

....

I sparked change in my schedule by:

....

....

....

....

DATE: ....

	I DID:	I FELT:

6:00 A.M. ....

6:30 A.M. ....

7:00 A.M. ....

7:30 A.M. ....

8:00 A.M. ....

8:30 A.M. ....

9:00 A.M. ....

9:30 A.M. ....

10:00 A.M. ....

10:30 A.M. ....

11:00 A.M. ....

11:30 A.M. ....

12:00 P.M. ....

NOTES

12:30 P.M. ....

1:00 P.M. ....

1:30 P.M. ....

2:00 P.M. ....

2:30 P.M. ....

3:00 P.M. ....

3:30 P.M. ....

4:00 P.M. ....

4:30 P.M. ....

5:00 P.M. ....

5:30 P.M. ....

6:00 P.M. ....

6:30 P.M. ....

7:00 P.M. ....

7:30 P.M. ....

8:00 P.M. ....

8:30 P.M. ....

9:00 P.M. ....

GET PRESENT

I am most productive during the hours of:

....

....

....

I am most creative during the hours of:

....

....

....

My body feels best when I move during the hours of:

....

....

....

I need rest during the hours of:
(NOTICE WHEN YOU FEEL TIRED/BORED DURING THE DAY, NOT JUST FOR SLEEP!)

....

....

....

....

MAKE AN IMPACT

I am able to prioritize my schedule by:

....

....

....

....

I burned down:

....

....

....

....

I sparked change in my schedule by:

....

....

....

....

The Time Frame I Want

THIS SECTION IS POSSIBLE TO COMPLETE BY:

....

DAYS - WEEKS - MONTHS

My three goals are:

- ....
- ....
- ....

The three most essential things I need to complete are:

- ....
- ....
- ....

The project that's possible:

....

....

....

....

CREATIVE UNTANGLING

The challenges I'm facing:

I can ask for help with:

Assumptions I'm making are:

BE INTENTIONAL

I want to feel:

....

EMOTION

My body needs:

....

....

....

....

I sabotage feeling the way I want by:

....

....

....

....

CLARITY THROUGH FULFILLMENT

The best ways to take care of myself this week are:

- ....

- ....

- ....

CREATE PURPOSE

Write what it's like at the end of this week:

WHAT DID YOU COMPLETE, WHAT SPARK DID YOU
LIGHT WITHIN, AND HOW ARE YOU CELEBRATING?

....

....

....

....

....

....

....

....

....

....

....

....

Use this grid to plan, organize, create, or unravel
whatever is needed for your projected time frame.

THINGS LIKE: MENU PLANNING, GROCERY LISTS, BUDGETING, GARDEN NOTES.
ANYTHING YOU NEED TO MOVE FROM CHAOS TO CREATION GOES HERE.

Today

....

Today's intention:

....

....

....

GET PRODUCTIVE

Today I will:

- ....

- ....

- ....

- ....

- ....

- ....

- ....

- ....

- ....

GET CREATIVE

I have an idea:

What will hold me back:

What I know is true:

One action I can take:

CONTINUE *Today* →

GET MOVING

I went to bed feeling:

....

....

....

I woke up feeling:

....

....

Moving made me feel:

....

MOVEMENT TYPE

DEPLETED   FULL

EMOTION TO ACTION

When I felt:

....

....

....

....

....

....

....

Action I took:

....

....

....

....

....

....

....

GET PURPOSEFUL

Today's affirmation:

....

....

Review your day from neutrality

WHAT WORKED: **WHAT DIDN'T WORK:**

● ....   ● ....

● ....   ● ....

● ....   ● ....

● ....   ● ....

● ....   ● ....

● ....   ● ....

● ....   ● ....

● ....   ● ....

My new choice:

....

....

....

Today

....

Today's intention:

....

....

....

GET PRODUCTIVE

Today I will:

- ....
- ....
- ....
- ....
- ....
- ....
- ....
- ....
- ....

GET CREATIVE

I have an idea:

What will hold me back:

What I know is true:

One action I can take:

GET MOVING

I went to bed feeling:

....

....

....

I woke up feeling:

....

....

....

Moving made me feel:

....

MOVEMENT TYPE

DEPLETED   FULL

EMOTION TO ACTION

When I felt:

....

....

....

....

....

....

....

Action I took:

....

....

....

....

....

....

....

GET PURPOSEFUL

Today's affirmation:

....

....

Review your day from neutrality

WHAT WORKED:

- ....
- ....
- ....
- ....
- ....
- ....
- ....
- ....

WHAT DIDN'T WORK:

- ....
- ....
- ....
- ....
- ....
- ....
- ....
- ....

My new choice:

....

....

....

Today

Today's intention:

....

....

....

GET PRODUCTIVE

Today I will:

- ....
- ....
- ....
- ....
- ....
- ....
- ....
- ....
- ....

GET CREATIVE

I have an idea:

What will hold me back:

What I know is true:

One action I can take:

CONTINUE *Today* →

GET MOVING

I went to bed feeling:

....

....

....

I woke up feeling:

....

....

Moving made me feel:

....

MOVEMENT TYPE

DEPLETED   FULL

EMOTION TO ACTION

When I felt:

Action I took:

....

....

....

....

....

....

....

GET PURPOSEFUL

Today's affirmation:

....

....

Review your day from neutrality

WHAT WORKED:

- ....
- ....
- ....
- ....
- ....
- ....
- ....
- ....

WHAT DIDN'T WORK:

- ....
- ....
- ....
- ....
- ....
- ....
- ....
- ....

My new choice:

....

....

....

Today

_____

Today's intention:

....

....

....

GET PRODUCTIVE

Today I will:

- ....
- ....
- ....
- ....
- ....
- ....
- ....
- ....
- ....

GET CREATIVE

I have an idea:

What will hold me back:

What I know is true:

One action I can take:

CONTINUE *Today* →

GET MOVING

I went to bed feeling:

....

....

....

I woke up feeling:

....

....

....

Moving made me feel:

....

MOVEMENT TYPE

DEPLETED   FULL

EMOTION TO ACTION

When I felt:

Action I took:

....

....

....

....

....

....

....

GET PURPOSEFUL

Today's affirmation:

....

....

Review your day from neutrality

WHAT WORKED: **WHAT DIDN'T WORK:**

- ....   - ....

- ....   - ....

- ....   - ....

- ....   - ....

- ....   - ....

- ....   - ....

- ....   - ....

- ....   - ....

My new choice:

....

....

....

Today

....

Today's intention:

....

....

....

GET PRODUCTIVE

Today I will:

- ....
- ....
- ....
- ....
- ....
- ....
- ....
- ....
- ....

GET CREATIVE

I have an idea:

What will hold me back:

What I know is true:

One action I can take:

CONTINUE *Today* →

GET MOVING

I went to bed feeling:

....

....

....

I woke up feeling:

....

....

....

Moving made me feel:

....

MOVEMENT TYPE

DEPLETED   FULL

EMOTION TO ACTION

When I felt:

Action I took:

GET PURPOSEFUL

Today's affirmation:

....

....

Review your day from neutrality

WHAT WORKED:

- ....

- ....

- ....

- ....

- ....

- ....

- ....

- ....

WHAT DIDN'T WORK:

- ....

- ....

- ....

- ....

- ....

- ....

- ....

- ....

My new choice:

....

....

....

Today

Today's intention:

....

....

....

GET PRODUCTIVE

Today I will:

- ....
- ....
- ....
- ....
- ....
- ....
- ....
- ....
- ....

GET CREATIVE

I have an idea:

What will hold me back:

What I know is true:

One action I can take:

CONTINUE *Today* →

GET MOVING

I went to bed feeling:

....

....

....

I woke up feeling:

....

....

....

Moving made me feel:

....

MOVEMENT TYPE

DEPLETED   FULL

EMOTION TO ACTION

When I felt:

....

....

....

....

....

....

....

Action I took:

....

....

....

....

....

....

....

GET PURPOSEFUL

Today's affirmation:

....

....

Review your day from neutrality

WHAT WORKED:

- ....

- ....

- ....

- ....

- ....

- ....

- ....

- ....

WHAT DIDN'T WORK:

- ....

- ....

- ....

- ....

- ....

- ....

- ....

- ....

My new choice:

....

....

....

Today

....

Today's intention:

....

....

....

GET PRODUCTIVE

Today I will:

- ....

- ....

- ....

- ....

- ....

- ....

- ....

- ....

- ....

GET CREATIVE

I have an idea:

What will hold me back:

What I know is true:

One action I can take:

CONTINUE *Today* →

GET MOVING

I went to bed feeling:

....

....

....

I woke up feeling:

....

....

Moving made me feel:

....

MOVEMENT TYPE

DEPLETED   **FULL**

EMOTION TO ACTION

When I felt:

Action I took:

....

....

....

....

....

....

....

GET PURPOSEFUL

Today's affirmation:

....

....

Review your day from neutrality

WHAT WORKED:

- ....

- ....

- ....

- ....

- ....

- ....

- ....

- ....

WHAT DIDN'T WORK:

- ....

- ....

- ....

- ....

- ....

- ....

- ....

- ....

My new choice:

....

....

....

CELEBRATE THE WINS

I ACHIEVED:

- ....
- ....
- ....
- ....

I TOOK CARE OF MYSELF BY:

- ....
- ....
- ....
- ....

I AM GRATEFUL FOR:

- ....
- ....
- ....
- ....

STEPS I TOOK THIS WEEK THAT HELPED ME ACHIEVE MY GOALS:

- ....
- ....
- ....
- ....

I learned:

....
....
....

CREATE WHOLENESS

This time I feel:

....

....

EMOTION

DEPLETED   FULL

I struggled with:

What I know is true:

I AM PRODUCTIVE.

I AM CREATIVE.

I MOVE WITH PURPOSE.

I LIVE WITH INTENTION.

After saying these affirmations, I now know to do:

....

....

....

....

....

....

....

....

Lighting a spark within takes something. But now that you've done it, what do you know you need to do to move forward into the possibility of your vision and goals?

....

....

....

....

....

....

....

....

....

stoke the fire

"WHEN I SEE PEOPLE STAND FULLY IN THEIR TRUTH, OR WHEN I SEE SOMEONE FALL DOWN, GET BACK UP, AND SAY, 'DAMN. THAT REALLY HURT, BUT THIS IS IMPORTANT TO ME AND I'M GOING IN AGAIN'—MY GUT REACTION IS 'WHAT A BADASS.'"
—BRENÉ BROWN

Think about the old-school way of stoking a fire: People used to use a hand pump to keep their fireplaces going so they didn't freeze to death or so they could cook their food. It takes work, and it takes practice to notice how much air you need to feed the fire.

That's where you are now, and you have to keep going because you can. Your fire might get out of control and it might almost go out; it's about noticing when you need more or less air.

Getting uncomfortable, questioning yourself, failing, and falling down are all parts of ambition. Notice during this section which ambitions you can choose for stoking possibility, and which ambitions you chose to let die out so that you can remain on your path to possibility.

The Time Frame I Want

....

DAYS - WEEKS - MONTHS

My three goals are:

- ....
- ....
- ....

The three most essential things I need to complete are:

- ....
- ....
- ....

The project that's possible:

....

....

....

....

....

CREATIVE UNTANGLING

The challenges I'm facing:

I can ask for help with:

Assumptions I'm making are:

BE INTENTIONAL

I want to feel:

....

EMOTION

My body needs:

....

....

....

....

I sabotage feeling the way I want by:

....

....

....

CLARITY THROUGH FULFILLMENT

The best ways to take care of myself this week are:

- ....

- ....

- ....

CREATE PURPOSE

Write what it's like at the end of this week:

WHAT DID YOU COMPLETE, WHAT DID YOU NEED TO KEEP
STOKING THE FIRE, AND HOW ARE YOU CELEBRATING?

Use this grid to plan, organize, create, or unravel
whatever is needed for your projected time frame.

THINGS LIKE: MENU PLANNING, GROCERY LISTS, BUDGETING, GARDEN NOTES.
ANYTHING YOU NEED TO MOVE FROM CHAOS TO CREATION GOES HERE.

Today

....

Today's intention:

....

....

....

GET PRODUCTIVE

Today I will:

- ....
- ....
- ....
- ....
- ....
- ....
- ....
- ....
- ....

GET CREATIVE

I have an idea:

What will hold me back:

What I know is true:

One action I can take:

CONTINUE *Today* →

GET MOVING

I went to bed feeling:

....

....

....

I woke up feeling:

....

....

....

Moving made me feel:

....

MOVEMENT TYPE

DEPLETED   **FULL**

EMOTION TO ACTION

When I felt:

Action I took:

....

....

....

....

....

....

....

GET PURPOSEFUL

Today's affirmation:

....

....

Review your day from neutrality

WHAT WORKED:

WHAT DIDN'T WORK:

- ....

- ....

- ....

- ....

- ....

- ....

- ....

- ....

- ....

- ....

- ....

- ....

- ....

- ....

- ....

- ....

My new choice:

....

....

....

Today

_____

Today's intention:

....
....
....

GET PRODUCTIVE

Today I will:

- ....
- ....
- ....
- ....
- ....
- ....
- ....
- ....
- ....

GET CREATIVE

I have an idea:

What will hold me back:

What I know is true:

One action I can take:

GET MOVING

I went to bed feeling:

....

....

I woke up feeling:

....

....

Moving made me feel:

....

MOVEMENT TYPE

DEPLETED   FULL

EMOTION TO ACTION

When I felt:

....

....

....

....

....

....

....

Action I took:

....

....

....

....

....

....

....

GET PURPOSEFUL

Today's affirmation:

....

....

Review your day from neutrality

WHAT WORKED:

- ....
- ....
- ....
- ....
- ....
- ....
- ....
- ....

WHAT DIDN'T WORK:

- ....
- ....
- ....
- ....
- ....
- ....
- ....
- ....

My new choice:

....

....

....

Today

Today's intention:

....

....

....

GET PRODUCTIVE

Today I will:

- ....
- ....
- ....
- ....
- ....
- ....
- ....
- ....
- ....

GET CREATIVE

I have an idea:

What will hold me back:

What I know is true:

One action I can take:

CONTINUE *Today* →

GET MOVING

I went to bed feeling:

....

....

....

I woke up feeling:

....

....

....

Moving made me feel:

....

MOVEMENT TYPE

DEPLETED   **FULL**

EMOTION TO ACTION

When I felt:

Action I took:

....

....

....

....

....

....

....

GET PURPOSEFUL

Today's affirmation:

....

....

Review your day from neutrality

WHAT WORKED:

- ....
- ....
- ....
- ....
- ....
- ....
- ....
- ....

WHAT DIDN'T WORK:

- ....
- ....
- ....
- ....
- ....
- ....
- ....
- ....

My new choice:

....

....

....

Today

....

Today's intention:

....

....

....

GET PRODUCTIVE

Today I will:

- ....
- ....
- ....
- ....
- ....
- ....
- ....
- ....
- ....

GET CREATIVE

I have an idea:

What will hold me back:

What I know is true:

One action I can take:

CONTINUE *Today* →

GET MOVING

I went to bed feeling:

....

....

....

I woke up feeling:

....

....

Moving made me feel:

....

MOVEMENT TYPE

DEPLETED   FULL

EMOTION TO ACTION

When I felt:

....

....

....

....

....

....

....

Action I took:

....

....

....

....

....

....

....

GET PURPOSEFUL

Today's affirmation:

....

....

Review your day from neutrality

WHAT WORKED:

- ....
- ....
- ....
- ....
- ....
- ....
- ....
- ....

WHAT DIDN'T WORK:

- ....
- ....
- ....
- ....
- ....
- ....
- ....
- ....

My new choice:

....

....

....

Today

Today's intention:

....
....
....

GET PRODUCTIVE

Today I will:

- ....
- ....
- ....
- ....
- ....
- ....
- ....
- ....
- ....

GET CREATIVE

I have an idea:

What will hold me back:

What I know is true:

One action I can take:

CONTINUE *Today* →

GET MOVING

I went to bed feeling:

....

....

....

I woke up feeling:

....

....

....

Moving made me feel:

....

MOVEMENT TYPE

DEPLETED   **FULL**

EMOTION TO ACTION

When I felt:

Action I took:

....

....

....

....

....

....

....

GET PURPOSEFUL

Today's affirmation:

....

....

Review your day from neutrality

WHAT WORKED:

- ....
- ....
- ....
- ....
- ....
- ....
- ....
- ....

WHAT DIDN'T WORK:

- ....
- ....
- ....
- ....
- ....
- ....
- ....
- ....

My new choice:

....

....

....

Today

....

Today's intention:

....

....

....

GET PRODUCTIVE

Today I will:

● ....

● ....

● ....

● ....

● ....

● ....

● ....

● ....

● ....

GET CREATIVE

I have an idea:

What will hold me back:

What I know is true:

One action I can take:

CONTINUE *Today* →

GET MOVING

I went to bed feeling:

....

....

....

I woke up feeling:

....

....

Moving made me feel:

....

MOVEMENT TYPE

DEPLETED   FULL

EMOTION TO ACTION

When I felt:

Action I took:

....

....

....

....

....

....

....

GET PURPOSEFUL

Today's affirmation:

....

....

Review your day from neutrality

WHAT WORKED:

- ....
- ....
- ....
- ....
- ....
- ....
- ....
- ....

WHAT DIDN'T WORK:

- ....
- ....
- ....
- ....
- ....
- ....
- ....
- ....

My new choice:

....

....

....

Today

Today's intention:

....

....

....

GET PRODUCTIVE

Today I will:

- ....

- ....

- ....

- ....

- ....

- ....

- ....

- ....

- ....

GET CREATIVE

I have an idea:

What will hold me back:

What I know is true:

One action I can take:

CONTINUE *Today* →

GET MOVING

I went to bed feeling:

....

....

....

I woke up feeling:

....

....

....

Moving made me feel:

....

MOVEMENT TYPE

DEPLETED   FULL

EMOTION TO ACTION

When I felt:

Action I took:

....

....

....

....

....

....

....

GET PURPOSEFUL

Today's affirmation:

....

....

Review your day from neutrality

WHAT WORKED:

- ....
- ....
- ....
- ....
- ....
- ....
- ....
- ....

WHAT DIDN'T WORK:

- ....
- ....
- ....
- ....
- ....
- ....
- ....
- ....

My new choice:

....

....

....

Reflection

CELEBRATE THE WINS

I ACHIEVED:

- ....
- ....
- ....
- ....

I TOOK CARE OF MYSELF BY:

- ....
- ....
- ....
- ....

I AM GRATEFUL FOR:

- ....
- ....
- ....
- ....

STEPS I TOOK THIS WEEK THAT HELPED ME ACHIEVE MY GOALS:

- ....
- ....
- ....
- ....

I learned:

....

....

....

CREATE WHOLENESS

This time I feel:

....

....

EMOTION

○ ○ ○ ○ ○

DEPLETED   FULL

I struggled with:

What I know is true:

I AM PRODUCTIVE.

I AM CREATIVE.

I MOVE WITH PURPOSE.

I LIVE WITH INTENTION.

After saying these affirmations, I continue to be:

....

....

....

....

....

....

....

Through success and through failure, through lighting sparks and stoking fires, you are multifaceted and capable of creating what's possible. Take a pause and bring into focus who you are through it all.

....

....

....

....

....

....

....

....

"BE SOMEBODY WHO MAKES EVERYONE FEEL LIKE SOMEBODY."
—KID PRESIDENT

It's time to shine. It's time to be somebody. Your possibility is a fire that will ignite the world.

As this journal comes to an end, reflect on the work you've done. Notice the fires you created and extinguished, and move from a vision to what's possible.

Give yourself permission to pause in this moment and celebrate. Get present to all you are and all you accomplished. Notice what you had to give up so you could get what you wanted in return.

You are courageous. You are capable. You are strong. It's time to ignite your fire and the world around you with your greatness and keep moving forward into what's possible.

I am most proud of:

....

....

....

....

....

....

....

I will continue to integrate what worked by:

....

....

....

....

....

....

....

One change I notice about myself is:

....

....

....

....

....

....

....

I want to remember:

....

....

....

....

....

....

....

In the time frame I chose, I accomplished:

....

....

....

....

....

....

....

What's next for me is:

....

....

....

....

....

....

....

....

Don't forget about all the work you just did. Are you moving into the possibility of rest, the possibility of ambition, or the possibility of both? You are allowed to pause and just be, if you need it.

....

....

....

....

....

....

....

....

....

....

....

....

....

....

....

....

....

ACKNOWLEDGMENTS

The Possibility Project could not have happened without the guidance, support, and encouragement from a number of people.

Thank you to my husband and children for encouraging me to be who I am fully, for loving me wholeheartedly, and reminding me to wake up every day and choose what's possible. I love you Big K, The Tiny Guy, and The Octopus.

Thank you to my dad, Luke "Gpa," for teaching me to sit at any table I choose, that my goals are limitless, and when there is only darkness all around you to choose life. I love you and YOLT (You Only Live Twice).

Thank you to my brother, Caleb, for being one of the most ambitious people I know and inspiring me to keep creating. You are the only person I will listen to say "just don't worry about it."

Thank you to my in-laws for always being so proud of me, for checking in, and for always accepting me.

Thank you to everyone at YESyoga, including staff, teachers, friends, and clients. The studio ignited something in me, especially after COVID; and you believed in me, you kept coming, and you supported saying YES for your life.

Thank you to Kynsey Creel and Ashley Miles for completing the initial version of this idea and giving me such great feedback to make this bigger than what it was.

Thank you to Ruby Privateer and The Collective Book Studio for helping me keep my feet on the ground through all of the changes, edits, and versions of this. Ruby, I knew you were meant to be when I heard your name; thank you for not letting me float away into the abyss.

Lastly, thank you to the random fortune-teller in Salem, Massachusetts, for telling me to write the book, an idea only a select few people knew about; if you read this, let me know what's next . . .